BLAST LAB
Rockets and Racers

For Izzy

DK
LONDON, NEW YORK,
MELBOURNE, MUNICH, and DELHI

Designed by Jess Bentall
Edited by Lisa Magloff and Penny Smith
Photography Guy Archard
Production editor Sean Daly
Jacket editor Mariza O'Keeffe

First published in Great Britain in 2009 by
Dorling Kindersley Limited,
80 Strand, London, WC2R 0RL

Text © 2009 Richard Hammond & September Films Limited
Layout and design © 2009 Dorling Kindersley Limited
A Penguin Company

2 4 6 8 10 9 7 5 3 1
BD706 – 01/09

All rights reserved. No part of this publication may be reproduced, stored in a retrieval system, or transmitted in any form or by any means, electronic, mechanical, photocopying, recording, or otherwise, without the prior written permission of the copyright owner.

A CIP catalogue record for this book is available from the British Library.

ISBN: 978-1-40534-081-6

Printed and bound by Graphicom, Italy

Discover more at
www.dk.com

A SEPTEMBER FILMS PRODUCTION in association with HAMSTER'S WHEEL PRODUCTIONS as seen on BBC.

BBC, CBBC and the BBC and CBBC logos are trademarks of the British Broadcasting Corporation and are used under licence. BBC logo © BBC 1996, CBBC logo © BBC 2007.

Balloon Hovercraft

AIR CAN BE USED TO POWER a mini-hovercraft that floats and GLIDES above the ground. Here's one we made earlier.

On the water

A hovercraft works best on a smooth surface, where there is LESS FRICTION to slow it down. Large hovercraft are often used on water as ferries or boats. The world speed record for a large hovercraft is 137.4 km/h (85.87 mph).

How does it work?

A hovercraft BLOWS OUT air under itself, making a kind of air cushion. This has enough pressure to support the weight of the craft and any passengers.

In a large hovercraft, a fan blows air under the hovercraft's platform, and the AIR IS TRAPPED between the platform and the ground by a piece of material called the skirt. A small amount of air leaks out from under the skirt, creating the cushion of air.

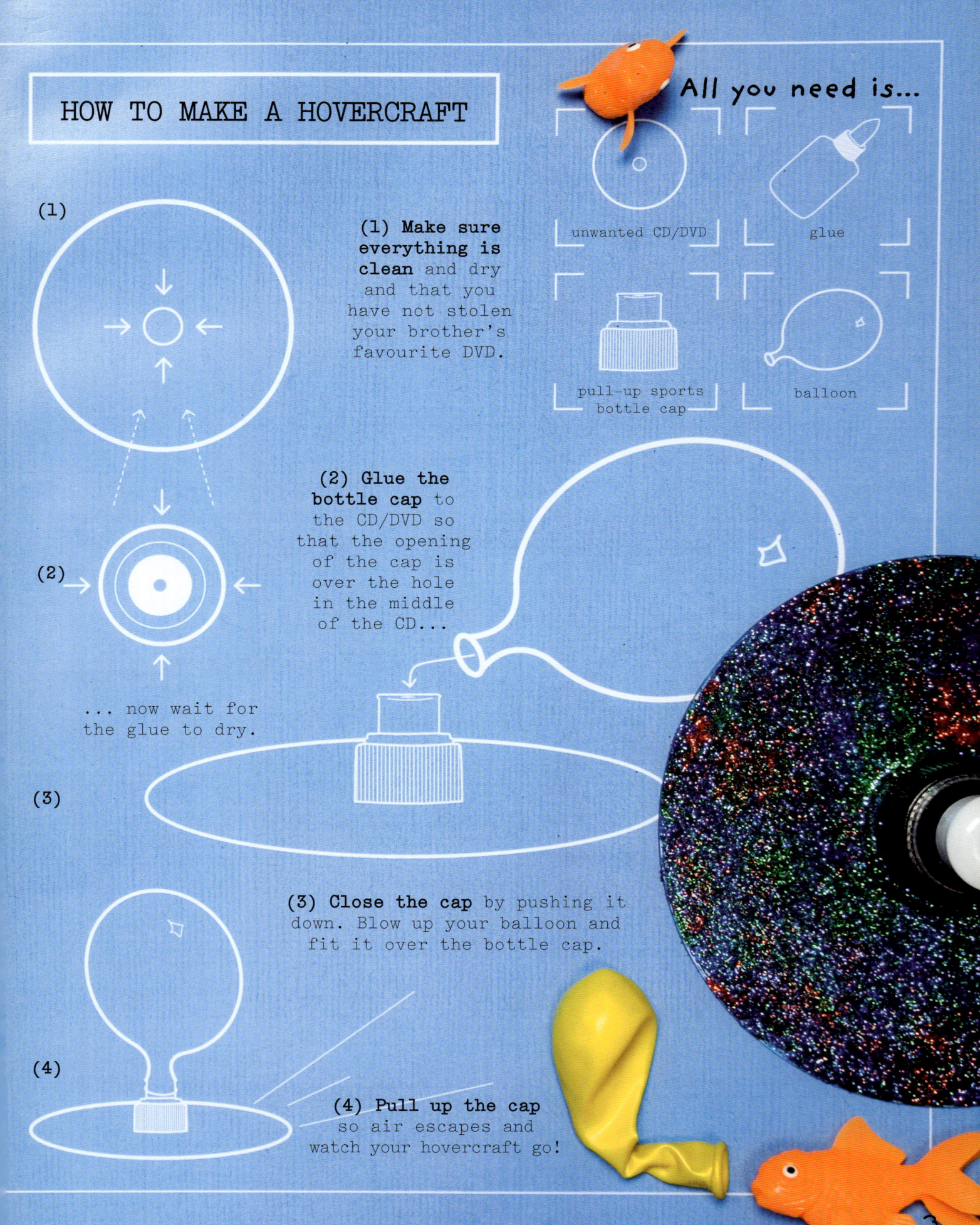

Reel Racer

With an elastic band as a POWER SOURCE, you can turn a cotton reel into a racer that zooms along at TOP SPEED!

How does it work?

When you twist the elastic band on a reel racer, you STRETCH THE BAND, which stores energy to do work at some future time. This is called potential energy.

The more you twist the elastic band, the more POTENTIAL ENERGY it has. As the elastic band unwinds, the potential energy changes into moving, or kinetic, energy, making the reel turn and move forwards.

Elastic-band energy

Here's something to try: make an elastic-band-powered car! You'll need a lightweight material (such as card) for the car's body, and REELS FOR WHEELS. And you'll need a really large elastic band to power the car. Experiment and see what happens.

HOW TO MAKE THE RACER

All you need is...

- cotton reel
- elastic band
- wooden skewers

(1) Slip the **elastic band** through the centre of the reel.

(2) Put a wooden skewer through one **loop** of the rubber band. Tape it in place. Break off the ends so they don't stick out.

(3) Push another skewer **through the other end** of the rubber band. Break it off so one end is flush with the edge of the reel and the other sticks out.

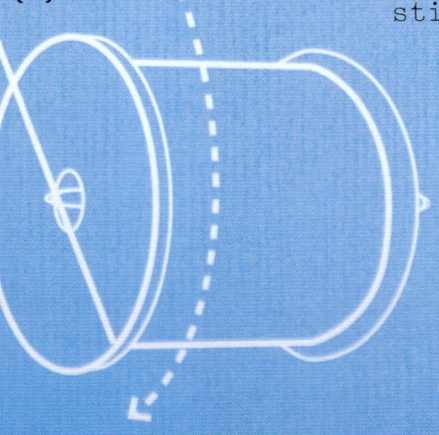

Wind the long skewer a few times and put the reel on the table. Let it go and... zoom! Off it races.

Boomerang

It spins as it FLIES. But will it come back to you? Make one and see.

MAKE A SPINNING CROSS

All you need is...

- card
- scissors
- pen

(1) Draw a shape like two plasters overlapping in a cross.

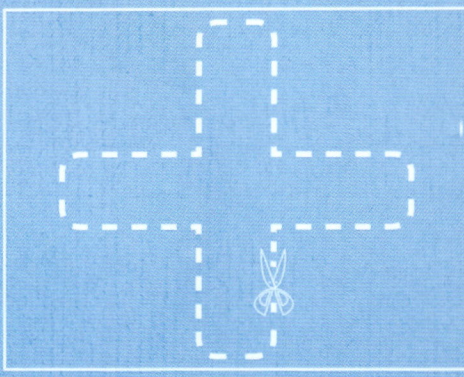

(2) Cut out the boomerang, and slightly bend all four arms upwards.

Now launch your boomerang!

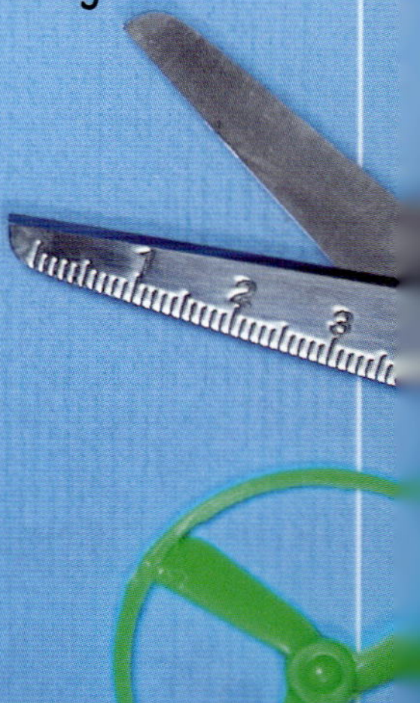

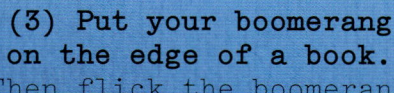

(3) Put your boomerang on the edge of a book. Then flick the boomerang with your finger so that it spins into the air.

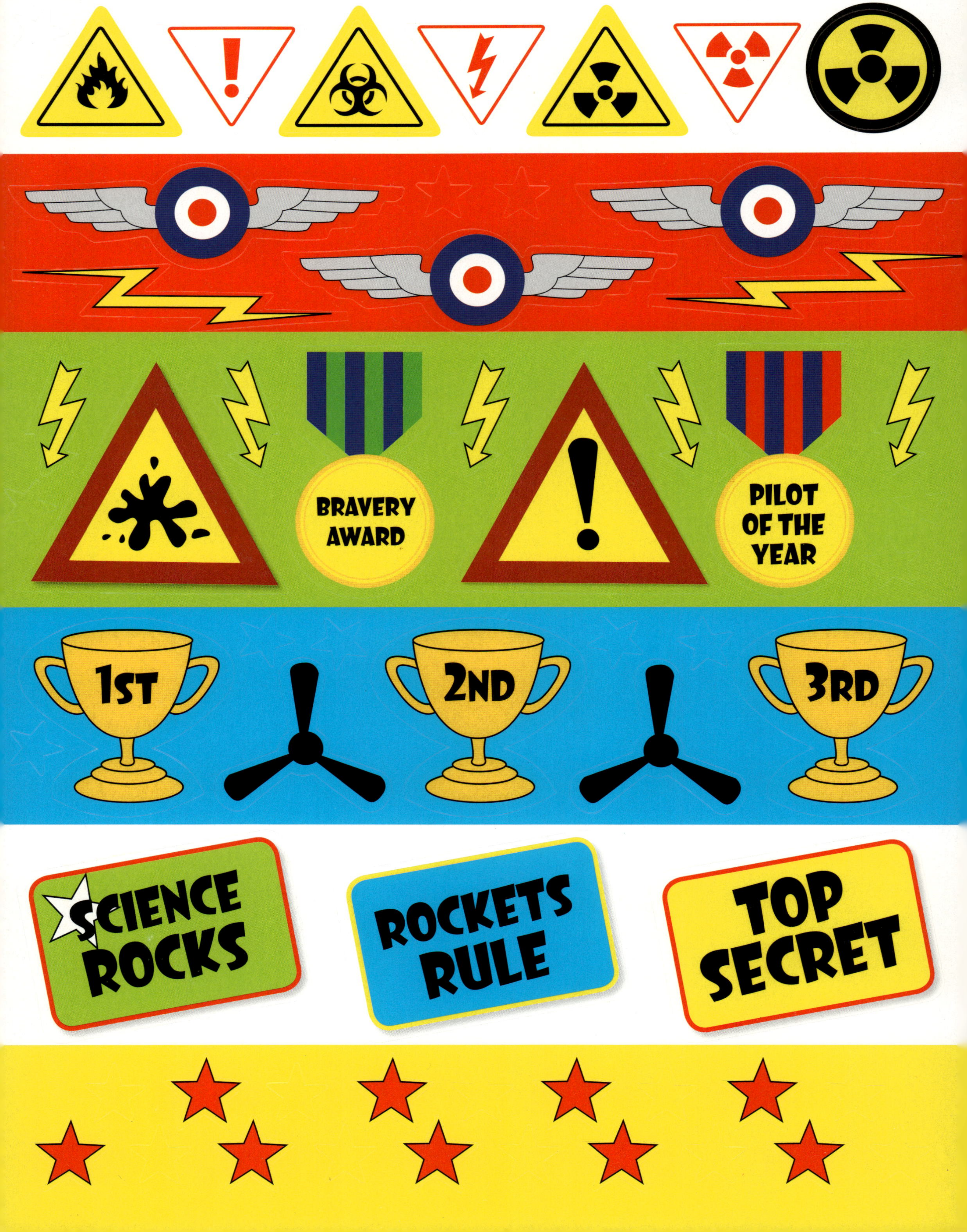
BRAVERY AWARD
PILOT OF THE YEAR
1ST
2ND
3RD
SCIENCE ROCKS
ROCKETS RULE
TOP SECRET

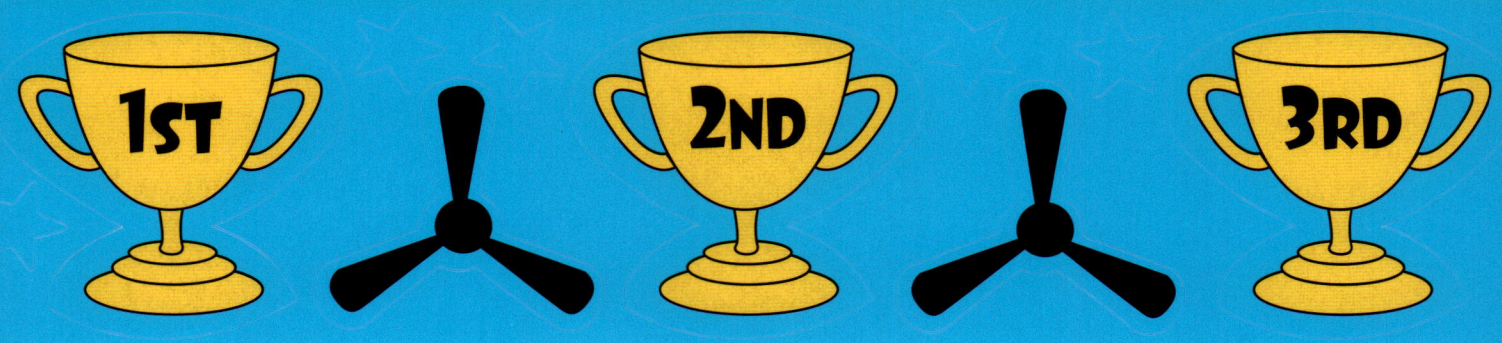

You can make this Flying "L" BOOMERANG from cardboard or an expired bank card (but ask Mum or Dad first!).

MAKE A FLYING "L"

All you need is...

card or bank card

scissors

(1) Cut the card into an L shape like the ones on this page.

(2) Hold the boomerang at the bend, then flick it with your finger.

← Now make it fly!

(3) If it doesn't fly back to you, try angling one wing upwards a bit more when you flick. And keep on practising!

How does it work?
As the boomerang spins, air flows faster over one wing than the other. This produces UNEVEN LIFT that tries to tip the boomerang over and gives it a curving flight.

11

Flying Crown

IT LOOKS MORE LIKE A HAT than a plane, but this flying crown is king of paper gliders. You might need a little practice... then you can make it fly a really long way!

How does it work?

As the crown moves through the air its top surface ACTS LIKE A WING. Some of its forward movement is turned into lift — a force that pushes the plane upwards.

(1) Fold a square piece of paper diagonally to make a triangle.

(2) and (3) Now fold over the longest edge by about 1 cm ($\frac{1}{2}$ in). Fold it over 3 more times.

(4) Twist round the long edge to make a circle. Make sure the folded part is on the inside of the circle.

(5) Join the circle together by pushing one end of the folded edge inside the other.

(6) Roll the point of the crown around a pencil, then unwind it so that it curls outwards. Cut a slit 2 cm (1 in) long into the curled point.

(7) Now throw your plane — hold it so the thin part of the circle faces downwards, and the point is to the back.

On the fly

The curve of the crown is the same sort of shape as a paraglider's wing. And paragliders are BRILLIANT at flying — they can travel as far as 160 km (100 miles) without an engine.

Cone Rocket

THREE, TWO, ONE, BLAST OFF! Here's how to make your own rocket — and launch it using a clever trick with air pressure.

HOW TO MAKE A ROCKET

All you need is...

- paper
- scissors
- tape
- wooden skewers (points broken off)
- straw
- plastic bottle
- Plasticine

(1) Draw a half circle on paper.

(2) Cut it out. Then twist it round into a cone shape (leaving a teeny hole at the tip). Tape it together.

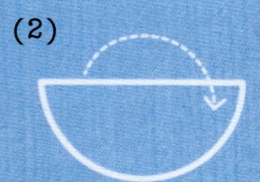

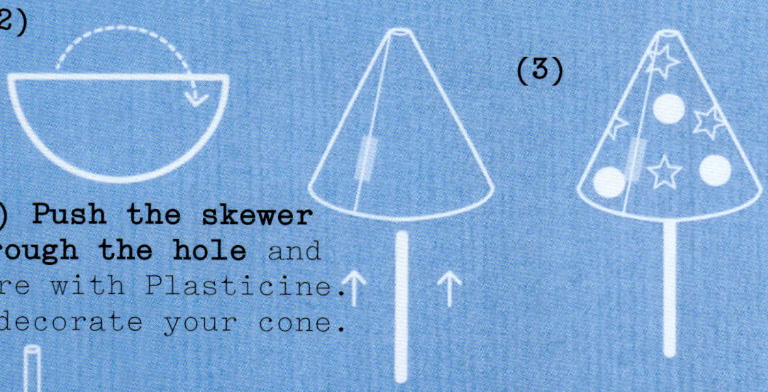

(3) Push the skewer through the hole and secure with Plasticine. Now decorate your cone.

(4) Put the straw into the plastic bottle so it sticks out 8 cm (3 in) or so. Secure with Plasticine, making sure the opening is sealed.

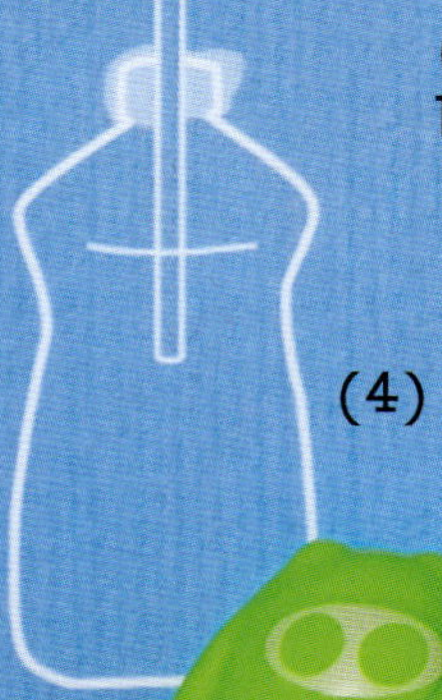

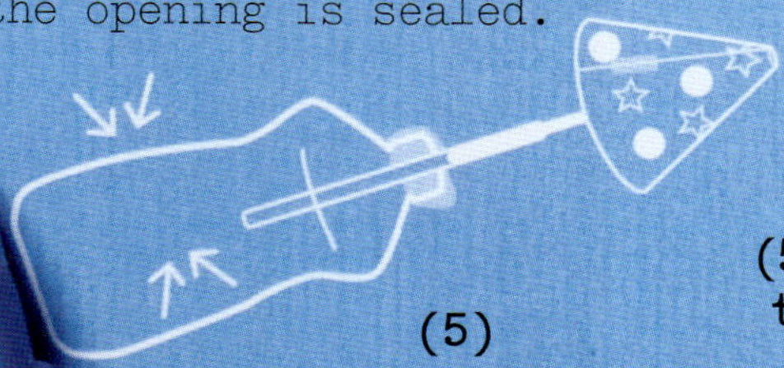

(5) Slide the wooden skewer into the straw in the bottle. Give the bottle a hard squeeze...

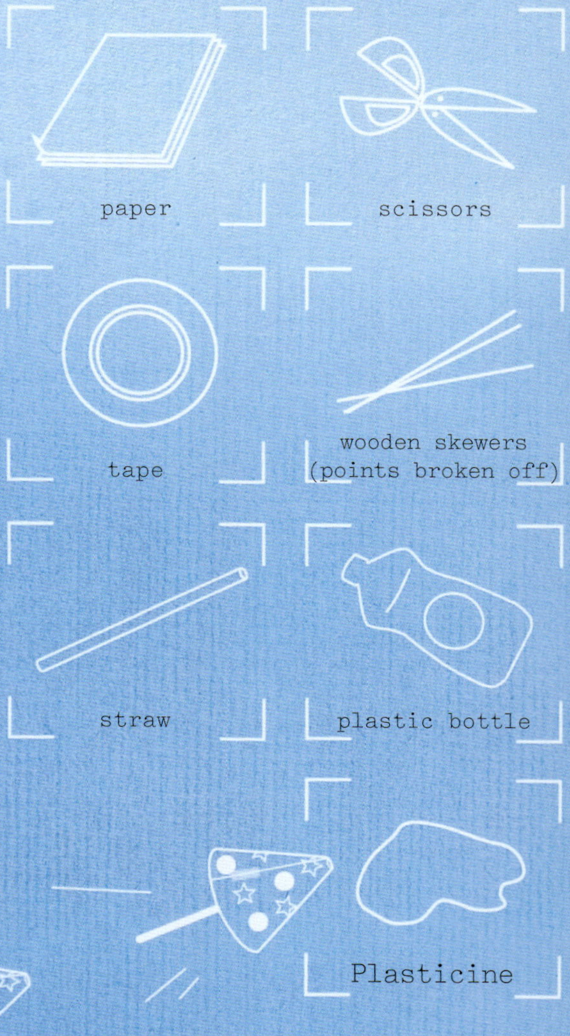

How does it work?

Even though you can't see air, you know it's there. Although air molecules are INVISIBLE, they still have mass and take up space — this means air has PUSHING POWER. In this rocket, the straw is the only way for air in the bottle to get out. When you squeeze the bottle, more pressure is put on the air inside. The air is forced out through the straw, making the rocket take off.

Are you under pressure?

The air in Earth's atmosphere is PRESSING against every little bit of you with a force of 1 kg per square centimetre (14.7 lbs per square inch). So why doesn't it squash you? Remember that you have air inside you too, and that air BALANCES OUT the pressure outside so you stay firm and not all squishy.

ZzApP!

WhoOSh!

... and WATCH THE ROCKET FLY!

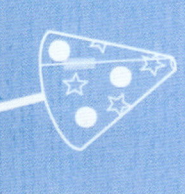

cRAsH!

Rockets & Racers Quiz

1. All the animals here have been sent into space. But which went first?

Cricket, mice, rats, frogs, newts, fruit flies, squirrel, snail, carp, monkey, dog, silkworms, toadfish, sea urchin, swordtail fish...

2. What's the world record for the flight of a paper aeroplane?

a. 6 m (20 ft)
b. 16.5 m (54 ft)
c. 34.14 m (112 ft)
d. 32 km (20 miles)

3. What is the land speed record for a wheeled vehicle?

a. 205 km/h (127 mph)
b. 565 km/h (351 mph)
c. 970 km/h (600 mph)
d. 1228 km/h (763 mph)

4. The oldest known boomerang is from which country?

a. Australia
b. Poland
c. India
d. China

ANSWERS: (1) b — Fruit flies were first, launched aboard a V2 rocket in 1947. (2) c — In 2007 Lucas Tortora set the record for distance and hang time of a paper aeroplane. His plane stayed up for 83 seconds. (3) d — 1228 km/h (763 mph) is the speed of the first wheeled vehicle to break the sound barrier. Answer "a" is the fastest steam-powered vehicle, answer "b" is the fastest motorcycle speed, and answer "c" is the speed of the first wheeled vehicle to break the sound barrier. (4) b — The oldest known boomerang was discovered in a cave in Poland. It was made of mammoth's tusk and is believed to be about 30,000 years old.